GW00992477

IRISH MAMMY

in your

POCKET

Sarah Cassidy & Kunak McGann

THE O'BRIEN PRESS
DUBLIN

First published 2019 by The O'Brien Press Ltd.,
12 Terenure Road East, Rathgar, Dublin 6, D06 HD27, Ireland.
Tel: +353 1 4923333; Fax: +353 1 4922777
E-mail: books@obrien.ie
Website: www.obrien.ie
The O'Brien Press is a member of Publishing Ireland.

ISBN: 978-1-78849-129-7

10 9 8 7 6 5 4 3 2 1
23 22 21 20 19

Layout and design: The O'Brien Press Ltd.

Printed and bound by Gutenberg Press, Malta.
The paper in this book is produced using pulp from managed forests.

Published in:

DUBLIN
UNESCO
City of Literature

I'll give you to the count
of three. 1, 2 ...

There's great drying out.

Were you born in a barn?

Did you hear who died?

How do you know
you don't like it if you
haven't tasted it?

As long as you live under
my roof, you'll live by
my rules.

You can hear when you
want to hear.

Just try it on.
No-one's looking.

You'll grow into it.

I don't care who started it,
I'm ending it.

It's all fun and games until
someone loses an eye.

If you're going to kill each
other, do it outside.

I'll light a candle for you.

Hot drop?

I'll put the kettle on.

Lord, give me strength.

When you get there,
ring twice.

I'll put a key under
the mat for you.

All you can do is your best.

I've put a hot water bottle
in the bed for you.

Turn off those lights!
Do you think I have shares
in the ESB??

Money doesn't grow
on trees.

Mary, Sean, Michael,
Gerard, Ann …
whatever your name is.

You're worth ten of him.

I have eyes in the back of
my head, you know.

It will only sting for
a second ...

You put the heart
crossways in me.

We won't stay long.

Are you wearing clean underwear? You could get hit by a bus.

We'll see ...

No cheese before bedtime – you'll have nightmares.

Are you getting up
for mass?

Don't go out with wet hair
or you'll catch your death.

What are you wasting your money on me for?

I won't come in, I'm like
the wreck of the Hesperus.

You look like you've been
dragged through a hedge
backwards.

Don't pick that dandelion
or you'll wet the bed.

Lord bless us and save us.

You poor thing, you're as sick as a small hospital.

A hot whiskey will sort
you right out.

Don't mind me,
I'm only your mother.

I'll have a pint of stout with
a dash of blackcurrant.
And don't forget my
half-pint glass.

What part of 'no' don't you understand?

If you haven't got
something nice to say,
don't say anything at all.

Your cousin's getting married tomorrow. Put the Child of Prague out.

Say a prayer to Saint
Anthony to find it for you.

Don't eat the seeds or
an apple tree will grow
in your belly.

Chewing gum stays in your stomach for SEVEN YEARS.

Sure, what else
would I be doing?

Would you leave your
brother alone?

Isn't it well for you?

Wash your mouth out
with soap.

Those are full of
the E numbers.

The ice-cream van only plays music when it's run *out* of ice-cream.

Jesus, Mary and Joseph
and all the saints.

You won't be happy until
you break that, will you?

Would you take my grave
as quick?

Don't be acting the maggot.

Are you off gallivanting
again?

Father Murphy does a
lovely funeral.

Don't sit on that radiator.
You'll get piles!

We'll see you on Sunday.
It's the Blessing of the
Graves.

No horseplay in the
good room.

Those biscuits are
for visitors.

What time do you call this?

Where do you think
YOU'RE going?

Feed a cold, starve a fever.

Don't eat with your
mouth open.

You're not going out
like that?!

Who'll be looking at
you anyway?

Everything happens
for a reason.

I can't hear myself think.

Who's 'she'?
The cat's mother?

Don't make me get the
wooden spoon.

Vegetables grown in the dark should be cooked in the dark.

Never mix the grape
and the grain.

Did you turn the
immersion off?

Don't walk away when
I'm talking to you.

Do you have change for
the church collection?

If Vinnie put his hand in
the fire, would you?

Would that be on the
internet, would it?

Have you checked RIP.ie?

That woman has shockin' notions.

It's far from cappuccinos
you were reared.

Eat that up. It'll put hairs
on your chest.

Eat your crusts and you'll
have lovely curly hair.

I said a decade of the
rosary for you.

There's post here for you.
Will I open it?

You're making a holy show
of yourself.

If there was work in
the bed, he'd sleep
on the floor.

Get out from under
my feet, will you?

She'd ask you what you
had for breakfast.

Good manners don't
cost a thing.

Don't sit so close
to the television.
You'll get square eyes.

I see Mary Ryan didn't go
up for communion.

A little birdy told me ...

I've had it up to *here*
with the lot of you.

What did your last servant
die of?

You'll get a cold in your kidneys in that get-up.

It's like talking to a
brick wall.

I haven't sat down all day.

Six o'clock and not a child
in the house washed.

I'll give you something
to cry about.

What's the magic word?

If you don't stop the fighting in the backseat, I'll pull over and you can all walk home.

I'm just popping out for a
few messages.

Close the door! We're not heating the road!

Take that coat off or it'll be
no use to you when you
go outside.

The Donegal postman
said we're to have a
grand summer.

Did you pack the
Factor 50?

I didn't ask who put it there,
I said 'pick it up'.

Beds are not made for
jumping on.

I'm not going to ask
you again.

Do you think we're made
of money?

That lad has one arm as
long as the other.

Sure she still has her communion money.

You're eating us out of
house and home.

No high jinx!

Take that face off of ye.

Don't you slam
that door.

Get out and stop
wasting the day!

Tell me this and tell me
no more …

Ask your father.

Wipe that smile off
your face.

You'll be better before
you're twice married.

What's meant for you
won't pass you by.

No telly till your
homework's done.

You'll sit there until
you've finished everything
on your plate.

Because I said so.
That's why.

There's no flies on you.

You don't get something
for nothing.

What way are you cutting
the sandwiches?
Those aren't triangles.

You treat this house
like a hotel.

I'm not running
a taxi service.

You're not hungry?
And all the starving
children in the world?

If I've told you once, I've told you a thousand times.

If I've to come up
those stairs ...

It's not off the ground
she licked it.

You kids have me up to 90.

Are you doing a line
with anyone?

He's no Gay Byrne.

There's a grand stretch
in the evenin'.

You'd better not be
wearing your good clothes!

What was the sermon
about?

Bring a coat with you!

If you fall and break
your legs, don't come
running to me.

He's Breda's son, you know Breda, she used to run the shop beside your Great Uncle Sean's house.

Use the back door.

In my day ...

Get into bed and I'll boil
up some 7-UP for you.

If the wind changes, your face will stay that way.

He has a face like a
wet weekend.

Eat your carrots and you'll see in the dark.

Mocking is catching.

I'll just have a
small Bailey's.

Bye, bye, bye, bye, bye.

Does your Mammy
take the biscuit?

1–30 mammyisms: Rich Tea.
Sure, she's still serving square sandwiches
to visitors. The shame.

31–80 mammyisms: Custard Cream.
She's been known to leave the immersion
on a couple of times. Tut tut!

81–120 mammyisms: Jaffa Cake.
She'll need to say a few more prayers to
Saint Anthony.

121–155 mammyisms: Viscount.
No-one boils 7-UP like this Irish Mammy!

About the Authors

Both children of 1980s Ireland, there's hardly a phrase in this book that Sarah and Kunak didn't hear from their own mammies growing up. But despite fair warning, they are frequently known to go out with their hair wet, steal the visitors' biscuits and go off gallivanting.

Sarah and Kunak co-wrote *The A to Z of Being Irish*, and Kunak is the author of *Red Rover, Red Rover! Games from an Irish Childhood*. They both work in publishing.